THE USES AND ABUSES OF
ECONOMIC PLANNING

T0346168

THE USES AND ABUSES OF ECONOMIC PLANNING

BY

SIR HUBERT HENDERSON

*Drummond Professor of Political Economy
in the University of Oxford*

THE REDE LECTURE
delivered in the University of Cambridge
on 9 May 1947

CAMBRIDGE
AT THE UNIVERSITY PRESS
1947

CAMBRIDGE
UNIVERSITY PRESS

University Printing House, Cambridge CB2 8BS, United Kingdom

Published in the United States of America by Cambridge University Press, New York

Cambridge University Press is part of the University of Cambridge.

It furthers the University's mission by disseminating knowledge in the pursuit of education, learning and research at the highest international levels of excellence.

www.cambridge.org
Information on this title: www.cambridge.org/9781107658530

© Cambridge University Press 1947

First published 1947
Re-issued 2014

A catalogue record for this publication is available from the British Library

ISBN 978-1-107-65853-0 Paperback

THE USES AND ABUSES OF
ECONOMIC PLANNING

THE idea of economic planning has become very popular in recent years. It is widely agreed, by many with enthusiasm and by others with a more reluctant acquiescence, that in Great Britain to-day we need a central economic plan. What is meant by this phrase is not always perfectly clear. It seems to mean somewhat different things to different minds. That, however, is more or less inevitable with a phrase which has acquired a sudden vogue; and, allowing for that, there is perhaps more reason to be surprised at the apparent measure of agreement as to what it means or should mean. But an idea may be incoherent, although there is little apparent dispute as to its content; and if an idea is incoherent, it may become mischievous, when the attempt is made to apply it unconditionally to practical affairs. It is high time, in my view, to subject this particular idea to close analysis.

Evidently, economic planning includes the idea of regulating by deliberate policy many matters which were formerly left to the laws of supply and demand, of relying less on impersonal economic forces and more on conscious organization than has been customary in the past. The idea of economic planning must comprise that as a minimum; and there are some who seem to mean by it not much more than that. They however are, I think, a small minority. Indeed, if that were all that the phrase 'economic planning' were intended to convey, it would perhaps be more appropriate to use quieter if longer words and to speak rather of the need for more State intervention and direction in our economic life. A second element forms an essential part of the content of planning as it seems most generally to be interpreted; that of quantitative programmes, the formulation in terms of precise statistics of the main objectives of economic policy. That is laid down as of the essence of central planning and control by Sir Oliver Franks in the lectures which he delivered in London on this subject and which have just been published in pamphlet form.[1] 'I think', he says, 'the essential elements are plans consisting of decisions of policy, quantitatively expressed in the form of programmes and such measures as in particular circumstances may be necessary to ensure the performance of these programmes.' Again, in the rather curious disquisition upon economic planning which forms the introduction

[1] Sir Oliver Franks, *Central Planning and Control in War and Peace*. Longmans, Green & Co.

to that best-seller White Paper, which appeared last February, known as the *Economic Survey for 1947*,[1] stress is laid on quantitative programmes and what are called 'economic budgets'. And there are phrases which imply that this White Paper, with its tables on Distribution of Resources and Distribution of Man-Power containing columns headed 1947 or December 1947, itself sets out at least a short-term plan.

But this raises another question as to the content of the idea. If ever we speak of making a plan in our personal affairs, we usually mean that we shall make definite arrangements for a longer period ahead than we might otherwise do. This 'looking ahead' is of the essence of the idea of planning in everyday life. It ıs natural, therefore, that many critics of the Government's White Paper should complain that a central economic plan, which is worthy of the name, cannot be limited to the current year, but must cover a period of years, four years or five years, on the analogy of the plans of Soviet Russia or Nazi Germany or of the Monnet Plan in France. The White Paper contains an apologetic paragraph in anticipation of this criticism:

The main emphasis so far has been laid upon comparatively short-term planning—planning for

[1] Cmd. 7046.

7

the next year ahead. This was the most urgent need—a guide to the vast number of decisions which had to be taken in the short-term allocation of resources. But exactly the same approach can be and is being applied to the longer-term problem, in order to secure a balanced development of the economy as a whole. It is too early yet to formulate the national needs over, say, a five-year period with enough precision to permit the announcement of a plan in sufficient detail to be a useful practical guide to industry and the public. There are still too many major uncertainties, especially in the international economic field. But a considerable amount of work is being done on these lines, in order to clarify the national objectives for a longer period ahead than is covered by this Paper, and to provide a framework for the long-term decisions of Government and industry.

I have quoted this paragraph in full, because of the light which it throws on the difficulties of the idea of economic planning, as currently interpreted. It is all very well to say that it is too early to formulate a statistical plan for five years because of 'major uncertainties, especially in the international economic field'. Have we any good reason to assume that those uncertainties will become materially less as time goes on? Is it likely to be easier to forecast the volume and value of our export trade even for a year or two ahead, when the present sellers' market has disappeared, and when the chances of international price competition may again exert a dominating influence on the flow of trade? And even if that question were to be answered Yes, on the ground of a vague belief that somehow things will gradually settle down, so that one year will be more like another than it is to-day, is it not for the unsettled times when matters cannot be expected to run smoothly of their own accord, that planning is said to be especially important? Evidently, there is a conflict between the *desideratum* that economic planning should relate to a considerable period ahead and the *desideratum* that it should consist largely of quantitative programmes. Yet, as we have seen, both these *desiderata* play a part in the idea of planning that is prevalent; and the idea which includes these warring elements makes a wide and strong appeal.

The strength of this appeal springs mainly from the belief that our economic and industrial achievement under war conditions was phenomenal. During the war, a very large part of our productive resources, more than half according to the accepted reckoning, was devoted to war purposes, to manning the Armed Forces and to supplying them with an immense range of costly equipment. Yet we succeeded somehow, with the remaining half of our productive power, in maintaining a tolerable standard of living, and for the poorest classes one that was higher on balance than they had known during peace. This suggests the moral that our productive resources were used far more fully and effectively during the war than they were previously, and the further moral that we might obtain a more satisfactory return from our exertions in time of peace, if we would apply to our peacetime economy methods of organization resembling those which served us so well in the war. Now much central direction by the Government, entailing the use of quantitative production programmes, was the outstanding feature of our wartime economic organization. This then is the principle (so runs the conscious or subconscious argument) which we should strive to apply, with suitable modifications, to the problem of securing increased prosperity in time of peace.

I shall not stop to inquire how far the belief which forms the basis of this argument is well founded, how far, that is to say, the apparent over-all achievement of wartime economic organization was a reality, or an illusion reflecting *inter alia* the quantitative importance of two branches of economic activity, which could be drastically curtailed for the duration of the war, but which are indispensable in the long run, namely, production for export, and the production of fixed capital goods, such as houses and generating stations. Upon that issue, I merely record my personal view that the apparent achievement was, in the sense indicated, largely an illusion, but did contain a significant element of reality. I am concerned at the moment with the psychological fact that by the end of the war, belief in the value of economic planning had taken root. At that time, moreover, this belief was accompanied by an optimistic assumption that the technique of planning was comparatively easy.

On the latter point, as distinct from the former, there has been a marked change of opinion over the last two years, and especially during the last few months. It has gradually become appreciated that there are greater difficulties in planning for prosperity in peace than in planning for efficiency in war; and in current pronouncements on the subject, insistence on the importance of economic planning is matched, and sometimes it seems overmatched, by stress upon these difficulties. First, it is pointed out that in peace the objects of planning are not so clear and simple as they are in war. 'In war', said the Lord President of the Council recently, 'there were two simple tests and two only: the needs of the fighting forces and the minimum needs of the civil population.

Today, there is a whole complex of needs, short-term and long-term, with the need to export cutting across all the others.' Therefore, it becomes more difficult to formulate clear plans. Secondly, the community is not bound together by the same unity of will and purpose, the same readiness to make sacrifices or to accept compulsion in the general interest; so that various methods which were used in war to aid in the carrying out of central economic policy, methods such as the direction of labour, the restriction of engagements, and industrial concentration schemes, are scarcely practicable in peace. Therefore, it is more difficult to execute any plans that may be formulated. These are the differences between the problems of wartime and those of peacetime economic planning on which attention has been chiefly focused in recent public discussion. They are important differences, undoubtedly. But I am not sure they are the most important ones; or at least that so stated they go to the root of the matter. There are two other differences, associated to some extent with those that I have mentioned, but deserving separate recognition, which have, in my view, an even more crucial bearing on questions as to the feasibility of planning and the type of planning that is appropriate in a peacetime economy. And it is to these two further differences, and to the implications which they carry, that I am chiefly anxious to invite attention.

The first of these differences is that during the war, the Government was the final purchaser, the effective consumer, of the munitions and war equipment which were wanted and were produced in greatly increased quantities; and the primary object of economic planning was to satisfy, as effectively as possible, this expanded Government demand. It was a practicable, though a highly complex task, to formulate the various Government requirements with precision, and to break them down, with increasing accuracy as time went on, into terms of the labour and materials which they would absorb. The supplies of labour and materials which could be made available set limits to the extent to which these requirements could be met, and among the requirements which had to be brought into the reckoning, though often as a very minor item, were the minimum needs of the civil population. These needs were therefore included within the scope of the elaborate programmes of quantitative allocation that were evolved.

But the impact of these allocation programmes upon the civilian market was simply that of a rationing of scarce supplies, a rationing that was

13

often both drastic and rough and ready. For commodities that are still in scarce supply, both raw materials and consumer goods, rationing systems are retained to-day with general acquiescence. This is what we term control. It is the sort of control, the need for which we all hope, not perhaps very confidently, will become progressively less extensive in future years. It is certainly not what enthusiasts mean by central economic planning. 'A real national plan', declares Mr Morrison, 'must be far more than a plan to ration scarce goods in the most sensible and far-sighted way; not a plan to make the best of poverty, but to increase prosperity.' The glowing hope which the idea of planning arouses in so many breasts is that it will prove an efficient instrument of expansion.

It is precisely here that the wartime analogy may be most deceptive. The plausibility of the notion that the technique of quantitative planning may help us to obtain increased prosperity in peace is derived from the success of this technique in promoting a great and rapid increase of war production. But this success depended on the fact that the Government was itself the consumer of the war products. The programmes of quantitative allocation were mainly concerned with the sorting out and satisfaction of Government requirements. Accordingly, to quote Sir Oliver Franks again:

These programmes were not estimates of need made by the intellect reviewing a situation, nor were they targets of aspiration springing from the heart; they were acts of will. Estimates of need were taken into account and attention was given to what was desirable, but the plan of allocation for a period was a directive to action.

I submit that it is only for commodities of which the State is the chief consumer that quantitative programmes can have this quality of 'acts of will' or 'directives to action' for purposes of increased consumption.

To-day, the State is the effective consumer or final purchaser of a considerable and increasing range of commodities which satisfy civilian needs —notably for the houses which are built under local authority housing schemes and for the plant required for the coalmines and other public utilities which are being nationalized. These are mostly fixed capital goods; and in the demand for such goods, the production of which forms the chief element in what is sometimes called investment, the State may now have come to play a predominant part. Therefore, in this section of our economy, there is scope and need for quantitative planning. It is certainly important that the

Government should frame definite programmes of the houses, the schools and the generating stations which they intend to build. It is important that they should compute as precisely as possible the calls which these programmes will make on man-power, materials and productive capacity, and that they should determine the magnitude of these programmes in the light of the economic situation as a whole, including the urgency of the need for consumer goods and services. There is scope, therefore, not only for detailed programmes relating to house-building, school-building and so forth separately, but for an over-all programme or budget for expenditure on fixed investment.

Here, however, I would interpolate a reservation. I have used the term 'fixed investment'. In my view, it is inexpedient for this purpose at least to lump long-term capital goods, such as I have been considering, in a common category with the machinery which is purchased by an ordinary industrial concern. That, of course, is what is usually done in economic analysis. A broad distinction is drawn between capital expenditure and current expenditure, which rests ultimately on the fact that the goods belonging to the former category yield their utility only gradually over a period of years and are therefore ordinarily financed from capital resources or borrowing, whereas the objects of current expenditure are consumed more quickly and are paid for out of income. Even from this standpoint, the distinction drawn is somewhat crude. A house, a school or a generating station lasts for a very long time; let us say for forty years or more. Much of the machinery used in industry becomes obsolete and is replaced after about seven years; and it must therefore earn a return sufficient to cover its cost comparatively soon. Some of the consumer goods which we regard as objects of current expenditure, our pots and pans, and in these days, our suits of clothes, last about as long. But apart from that, I suggest that the difference between forty years and seven is quite as significant as the difference between seven years' life and immediate consumption. Considerations of a more practical order are also pertinent. The State is not the chief buyer of machinery, as it is of longer-term capital goods. Moreover, these two classes of capital goods absorb largely different materials and are produced by different industries, which differ markedly to-day in their capacity to undertake additional work.

For these reasons, I contend that the national investment budget should be a really long-term investment budget, relating only to the most durable types of capital goods; and I attach

17

considerable importance to this matter. It may be desirable in the interests of economic balance to restrain within moderate limits the amount of long-term investment work that is set on foot during the next few years. There are *not* equally good reasons for slowing down the work of renewing and modernizing industrial plant. Considerable confusion of thought has been caused, and policy may conceivably be distorted, by the lumping together in the White Paper calculations of these two different types of capital goods.

But that is somewhat of a digression and I return now to my main argument. Outside the important sector of investment work, the role of the State as the final purchaser of non-military goods is still a very minor one. It follows, I submit, that over the greater part of the economic system, quantitative programmes cannot play the part of 'directives to action' for purposes of increasing prosperity.

I pass to my second proposition. During the war it was permissible and necessary to disregard, for the time being, certain objects of policy which are of cardinal importance in peace. I refer in particular to three: first, the balancing of the budget; second, equilibrium between savings and investment, if I may be indulged in putting it that way; and third, equilibrium in the balance of international payments. Upon all those matters, the exigencies of war entitled and compelled us to take what was in one sense a short-sighted view. The paramount necessity was to win the war; and it would clearly have been wrong to have refrained from doing anything helpful to that end, because of post-war disadvantages, however serious. Therefore, among other things, we ran through our accumulated dollar assets and incurred heavy external indebtedness in the form of sterling balances owned abroad.

That is not a process which can possibly continue indefinitely; and indeed, there can be no two opinions as to the crucial importance in time of peace of living within our international income and of adjusting accordingly the balance between our imports and our exports. This relates to the third objective. If the other two are disregarded in time of peace, inflationary conditions may be perpetuated, carrying with them many dangers, including the one which recent events have brought home to us—that stocks of industrial materials and components may become insufficient to sustain continuous production.

Now each of these cardinal objectives of economic policy is concerned with a relation: not with one thing but with the balance between two. The kind of help which quantitative programmes can give is greatly affected by that fact. Consider first the task of balancing the budget. There the Government is in effective control of both sides of the account; and both can be and are expressed in precise quantitative terms. It rests with the Chancellor of the Exchequer and his colleagues to determine how much expenditure shall be allowed; and within the limits of the national taxable capacity, it is within their power to impose taxation sufficient to yield a corresponding revenue. The essential objective, however, is not to raise so much revenue or to keep expenditure down to a certain sum, but to keep the two in balance. True, it makes a great difference whether this balance is struck at a high level of revenue and expenditure or at a low level of both. Accordingly, past Chancellors have frequently declared it to be their aim to reduce expenditure and taxation to a lower level, and have occasionally been rash enough to specify the magnitude of the reductions which they hope to achieve over a period of years. When they have done that, they may be said to have set up targets defined in quantitative terms; and such targets may be of some use as guides or spurs to action, though history does not record that they have usually been reached. But they are essentially different from the quantitative programmes of wartime

20

planning with their quality of directives to action. The parallel to the latter is supplied by the yearly Estimates and Finance Act. Thus, even in this financial sphere, where the Government is, as I have said, in effective control of both sides of the account, we see that quantitative programmes which represent acts of will are short-term and that any long-term programmes have the more dubious character of targets.

Let us turn now to the task of securing equilibrium in the balance of international payments. Here the immediate problem is that of closing a large gap between the two sides of the account. There are two ways of doing this, to cut down our overseas expenditure and to increase our overseas income; and so long as the costs of occupation forces and similar quasi-wartime Governmental disbursements play an important part in the total of our overseas expenditure, it is clear that we must attack the problem from both ends. As compared, however, with the pre-war position, it is undoubtedly preferable to close the gap so far as we can by restoring our income rather than by reducing our expenditure, which means by increasing exports rather than by curtailing imports. It is of value, therefore, to have the calculation with which we are all familiar, that we must increase our exports by 75 per cent in volume above the level of 1938 if we are to import as much as we did before the war. That supplies us with a target which may be useful as a guide to policy.

But again this cannot be a directive to action. Nor is it possible for a short-term export programme, relating only to a single year, to have this quality. Here the point is important that for the balance of payments problem, the Government is not in effective control of both sides of the account. It can encourage and stimulate exports by various means; but since it is not the purchaser of the exports, it cannot determine their volume. It cannot do so even in a sellers' market when the limiting factor is production. Still less will it be able to do so when the limiting factor becomes the difficulty of finding purchasers abroad. Then the determining influences will be in part the prosperity and policies of countries overseas which are our customers, and in part the relation of costs and prices in Great Britain to those in countries which are our chief competitors.

The size of the export trade which we shall be able to maintain in these circumstances must be uncertain and unstable, liable to large fluctuations from year to year. Indeed, in the years that lie ahead, this uncertainty and this instability may be exceptionally great, in consequence of the dislocating impact of a total war upon the world economy. If international obligations do not prevent, it might be possible to do a great deal to limit the scope of the probable fluctuations and to introduce an element of reliability and steadiness into the flow of foreign trade by planned arrangements; for example, bilateral trade agreements between particular countries providing for the interchange of prescribed minimum quantities of each other's goods. Bilateral trade agreements of this sort belong to the category of quantitative programmes that can be carried out. But a main object of the conference upon commercial policy which is now in session at Geneva is to forbid such bilateral trade agreements altogether, and to work towards the elimination of other practices which qualify the power of international price competition to swing trade from one channel to another. Among these practices is the system of preferential import duties within the British Commonwealth, which has contributed towards reliability and steadiness. The principle of non-discrimination, to which the conference on trade policy is dedicated, is indeed fundamentally incompatible with the principle of planning in the sphere of external trade. Planning implies that you choose; non-discrimination that you must not choose.

A curious paradox is worth noting here. The ideology which seeks to put the flow of international trade more completely than before the war at the mercy of the chances and vagaries of international price competition is accepted by many, though certainly not by all, of the strongest advocates of planning in our internal affairs. The inconsistency is to be explained by the spell still cast by the great Free Trade tradition. That tradition comprised two elements: first, a belief in the value of international trade, and second, the belief that international trade will be best conducted if Governments do not interfere with it. For Great Britain, the first of these elements, the judgement as to the value of international trade, remains true and vitally important. But the second proposition becomes much more doubtful in conditions of extreme disequilibrium in the international economic world, and in these days when we are trying to regulate so much else. I do not believe that it will be possible to regulate our internal economy effectively, much less to plan it, if our external economy is left unregulated. Indeed, as I shall suggest in a moment, the continued regulation of our external economy seems to be inevitable on the import side of the account.

On the export side, however, our freedom of action is already seriously circumscribed by the conditions of the Anglo-American Loan Agreement and may perhaps be circumscribed still more in future. Even if it were otherwise, the extent to which the volume of exports could be determined by planned arrangements would be limited; and questions of costs and prices would still be vital. As matters are, the Government will best serve the purpose of an adequate export trade, if the general policy which it pursues is such as to promote industrial efficiency and to help to maintain costs and prices at a competitive level. In the effort to overcome our export difficulties, there will be need, I am sure, for many contacts and much co-operation between Government and industry; but it is an illusion, I fear, to suppose that any good can be done by formulating annual global export programmes and calling on industry to fulfil them. There may even be a danger that such programmes, which can only have the significance of wishes, may be treated as a substitute for the necessity for disagreeable action, that they may serve as a smoke-screen under cover of which the crucial questions of costs and prices and competitive efficiency are evaded.

Our essential objective, in the field of international payments, is to effect a large change in our import-export balance. In so far as we cannot do this by increasing exports, we must do it by curtailing imports; and here the Government is in a position to control events more effectively. Here, therefore, may be scope and need for quantitative programmes bearing the character of instruments of policy. In my judgement, we must expect that such programmes will be necessary for an indefinite future. I form that judgement, not only because of my sense of the difficulties of increasing our exports very greatly, but also because the link which used to connect the supply of internal purchasing-power with the volume of our monetary reserves has been severed, almost certainly for good. Our internal purchasing-power will probably be maintained at a level which would cause us to import much more than in 1938 if imports were entirely unchecked. Hence an indefinitely continuing need for quantitative programmes of import restriction. But there is no place for a long-term target on this matter. The restrictions, however necessary, will be restrictions of the irksome type, which we should all wish to diminish as much as possible. For completeness I should add, under this heading, that a more positive and expansionist purpose might possibly be served by medium-term contracts for the purchase of some of the staple foodstuffs and raw materials which we import. But this is a large and controversial question into which I cannot enter now.

It will be apparent from what I have said so far that the term 'quantitative planning' is often used loosely to include two very different things: first, quantitative programmes which are what Sir Oliver Franks calls 'directives to action', and second, rough and ready statistical targets. My general contention is that in peace, the scope for the former is very limited, except for the unwelcome though often necessary purpose of adapting ourselves to scarcity, and that the latter can only help by indicating the kind of policy which may be needed.

But there is a third type of statistical calculation which is also mixed up with the idea of quantitative planning entertained by some—namely, the so-called 'model' type of comprehensive forecast. The distinguishing feature of this type of calculation is that it is hypothetical in the extreme. It first builds an elaborate algebraical apparatus to indicate the various factors which will combine to determine the matters which are being forecast, and then attempts to evaluate these factors in the light of such data as may be available. The intellectual ingenuity which goes to this work is often impressive; but for any practical purpose in the sphere of central economic policy, the method has the serious defect that the factors which are of dominating importance are often quite unpredictable, though the consequent unreliability of the final result is hidden from spectators by the massive bulk of the apparatus employed. Moreover, in the process of guessing the key factors, a sort of Gresham's Law is apt to operate, under which wishful thinking drives out common sense.

These defects are well illustrated by the 'model' calculation made by Mr Nicholas Kaldor three years ago, which was published as an Appendix in Lord Beveridge's book, *Full Employment in a Free Society*, and was acclaimed at the time as a brilliant example of this method. Mr Kaldor forecast that assuming that the war would end as it did in the summer of 1945, our productive capacity in Great Britain would be sufficient in 1948 to achieve the following objects:

(1) To enable us to consume 19 per cent more consumers' goods and services than we did in 1938—19 per cent more; not, it may be noted, a rough 20 per cent.

(2) To raise real investment activity to 25 per cent above the pre-war level.

(3) To eliminate completely the deficit in our international balance of payments.

(4) To balance the budget with rates of taxation only 6 per cent on the average above those of 1938.

This was an agreeable vision.[1] In times of strain and difficulty it is always agreeable to escape from actualities into the realms of fancy; and Mr Kaldor's fairyland picture of a notional 1948 may perhaps be regarded as an analogue to Sir Thomas More's *Utopia* or William Morris's *News from Nowhere*, in a medium appropriate to an 'age of sophisters, economists and calculators'. But if used as instruments of central economic policy, calculations of the 'model' type are unlikely in my view to do more than provide model dwellings for a Fool's Paradise.

More generally, I suggest that current notions about planning exaggerate greatly the aid which economic policy can receive from quantitative calculations relating to the future. It is all very well to say that the objects of policy should be precisely defined; or else action will be confused and ineffective. In peacetime, as I have tried to show, the central objectives of policy must be those of equilibrium or balance, not absolute mag-

[1] Of the various over-optimistic assumptions that contributed to its creation, the most important was that in 1948 average output per person employed in Great Britain would be 13 per cent *higher* than it was in 1938. In fairness to Mr Kaldor, it should be said that his cheerfulness in 1944 upon this matter was in no way peculiar to him, but appeared at the time to predominate among economists and statisticians. This makes it the more pertinent, however, as an example of the psychological Gresham's Law to which reference has been made.

nitudes. Indeed, if I were asked to state in a single word the goal to which economic policy should be directed in Great Britain at the present time, I should answer, Balance; balance in the matters I have already mentioned, the budget, international payments, between savings and investment; but balance also in other matters, between primary and secondary production, in the labour market, and above all between aggregate demand and aggregate supply in the economic system as a whole. Balance in all departments of economic life is an essential condition of attaining a high level of productivity and material well-being.

The practical implications of the importance of balance are, however, not always palatable; and dislike of these implications seems to form in some minds the psychological basis of an exaggerated estimate of the virtues of planning. I have already referred to the danger that reliance on quantitative export programmes may distract attention from the price and cost conditions essential to the maintenance of an adequate export trade. This danger is not limited to the export field. A striking feature of the *Economic Survey for* 1947 was its disregard, virtually complete, of forces of supply, and demand, and of the influence which they may exert on the attainment of the objectives stated. You might almost suppose that the time-honoured forces have ceased to operate in the modern world. The view that we should not allow impersonal economic forces to exert the absolute sway over our economic life that they once did, nay that we should treat them as our servant instead of our master, is one to which I wholeheartedly subscribe. But to ignore them is stupid. They are actively at work to-day and our present economic troubles are partly due to the fact that they are working in directions which are ill-suited to our needs. In the labour market, for example, by drawing workpeople away from more essential to less essential occupations, they are largely responsible for what we call the mal-distribution of our man-power. To create conditions under which these forces will work more to our advantage should be a main preoccupation of economic statesmanship.

Nothing that I have said is intended to combat the view that we must have more State intervention and direction in our economic life than we had before the war. If the phrase 'economic planning' is given only what I described at the outset as its minimum content, I believe in economic planning. Nor have I any dislike of quantitative programmes, wherever they are appropriate, as for certain purposes, notably the regulation of imports, they undoubtedly are. We are faced in this country with the need to effect large-scale readjustments in several branches of our economic affairs; and I do not believe in the light of experience that large-scale readjustments will be made smoothly or satisfactorily if they are left to the forces of supply and demand, unaided and uncontrolled. Indeed, I have been partly moved to explore this particular subject on this occasion by the apprehension that disillusionment, following attempts to apply muddled notions about planning, may cause a reaction towards *laissez-faire* doctrine and practice which might prove unfortunate in the extreme. In overcoming our many difficulties, we may derive real help from planned arrangements of various sorts. The danger against which this lecture is designed as a warning is that, on the strength of the misleading analogy of our wartime experience, planning may be regarded as a magic talisman by which those difficulties can be charmed away.

www.ingramcontent.com/pod-product-compliance
Ingram Content Group UK Ltd.
Pitfield, Milton Keynes, MK11 3LW, UK
UKHW042141280225
455719UK00001B/25